I0176570

Beat, Writings & Ramblings

By

William P. Haynes W Elliot

Raggedy Ann

Scar covered tracks in the house of delight, trying to conform and survive. Still crawling from her

Father's liquored embrace when she was only four years old. A hurtful memory worn behind bitter

Eyes. Placing the money in the small wooden hutch; She tells the john it will cost extra for: and

Recites a list as she undresses before a dusty mirror. Drunk and cruel the man knocks her down

Roughly to the bed. "Kitten," he whispers. The same nickname that her father used ten years ago.

She lunges for the hutch, tears drowning the hurt. Frantically drawing a knife from the drawer, she

Strikes at the bitterness of memories. At first the john laughs until he brings his arm back to hit her

and sees his blood pooling on the floor. "Daddy!" she screams. "You bitch!" he answers.

Slowly he releases his grip on her hair and staggers back against the wall. She stares as he sinks to his knees, pleading with her to get help; She steps by him and walks to the hutch. Taking out a torn

Raggedy Ann doll, she sits back down by his feet. "Why don't you love me daddy?" "Please for God's

Sakes, get help" Clutching her doll closely to her heart she walks out of room and into the darkness

Of the deserted New York city streets that wait like forgotten lovers three stories below.

THE JOB

Johnny was from Akron
    Met him in Haiphog
    Got us drunk and red-light fevered
    During the bombing of Hanoi in 1972
    Getting higher than shit during the mining
    Of the northern ports. We toked to the demise
    Of Ho Chi Minh and the peace talks in Paris.
    72 remembered by nothing' but death and
    'Light my fire'
    I found him in the Nghe An province in late august
    Blown to pieces. Asked me to finish the job.

HOLY WARS

Burma's Tin Hle
   13 years old
   Killing machine
   Karen's Palu Ke
   15 years old with
   One of his legs shot off
   Afghanistan, Northern Ireland
   Burma, Islam Dara
   The children of Rambo the holy war
   Wrapping their wounds in the bandages of Gods
   Their tongues in the lies taught by their fathers
   Field stripping AK-47s over the graves of children
   Who were slower to learn while their fathers earn money
   Unloading the weapons supplied by the CIA and the Russians
   Boys with the glassy eyed stare of men who've seen too
   Much death
   Men with tears of childhood holding their sons
   The CIA and the Russians in the background counting the
   Spoils
   THE HOLY WAR?

I AM FABULOUSLY RICH TODAY

My pockets filled with bleached sand dollars
    Silver eucalyptus quarters diamond-flecked mica chips
    Golden boughs of sea-oats and pine-nut tender
    Solar power warms my day, then incandescent moonlight
    Showers rays illuminating the waters.
    Phosphorescence dazzles my senses as I
    Watch the sparkling water ballet choreographed
    By mullet whisker cats and trout that via for center
    Stage my books are flat sea-grape leaves gossip spread
    By the ever fashion critical jays telepathed by leaping porpoises
    Then echoed in curled virginal chambers of striped nautilus shells
    I am abundantly rich today, a connoisseur dining on nature;
    Pink fleshed shrimp, succulent scallops & clams
    Nourishment for my body as the panoramic flourish
    And you
    Bring succor to my soul

DIANE

I walk the distance between us on burning coals
Straddle the high wire between mountains for the
Memory of your eyes/blue/green
Like the blanket spread over sands
In the wee hours of never, where dreams fell
Like shards of shattered clouds And I knelt before you
Spellbound, never fathoming the keenness of your lonely
Sad/soul/spirit and we left still a distance from understanding
Your woman needs, unanswered by everyone
Like a soul song fading so softly on a night breeze

LIKE A RAVAGED LENNY BRUCE

It's like the old west out there
With kids with Tech-9's drawing down
But they are polite and hand back the empty
Wallets to the subway riders on the Avenue A line
After cleaning them out of cash and jewelry.

And even mother nature has turned bad-assed
Flooding the mid-west, heating up the north and
Hitting Japan with earthquakes
Anyone out there remember the apocalypse?
Does it come with thunder or the whimper of a
Dying beast, a T-Rex
King of the kingdom or so he thought until he got
His ass reamed or hers not to be sexist about extinction
And everyone laughs except those with AIDS
It can't happen here as Zappa said; because I've
Been checking it out baby and it can't happen here.
Because you have a swimming pool and you're white?
And my friend got drunk and took it up the ass from
Somebody but in the end if we are
all positive what the fuck difference does it make
In the end[end] cause dead smells the same on all of us and that is
what
Makes us all the same that smell that fear that you aren't going to
hear

The ocean again, share a secret, taste somebody else's salty
tears

And tell them it's going to be alright. Maybe George Dowden is correct

Maybe I am a ravaged Lenny Bruce

VENTURA BLVD

Stars play so pretty in your hair
As you lose your gravity to my heart
Planet spin lazily in the contours of your eyes
If I remove the mask will we be able to breathe together?
And if we are pulled apart would the universe
Fade out?
On the moon I promise you the earth and mean it.
You laugh. I am very much in love until very much in love
Becomes a poem, very much in love, very much in love
Very much in love. Our love is the poem, every line, every
Word. You laugh I love. I remember when I held the door
For you. I remember when I offered you my seat.
I remember when you took it. The seat was my poem, my
Poem to you; better than a carving on a tree. The seat ran on
Petrol, drove around town, a mobile poem.
My poem just drove down Ventura Blvd; since we broke up
It searches for other poems. I wish it luck.

POEM FOR L<M<

I must have come too close to tearing the veil
From your eyes Too have asked you to cross a bridge
When the distance was greater than either of us imagined
Now I wait on the other side listening to sparrows and doves
But the truth is; I hear only silence your heart beating
someplace
That I'll never find

THE LAST GREYHOUND

It was midnight in L.A.
A lifetime from the Drake
"Stayin or going?" the driver asked.
I touched the lights with my hands
Like a thousand stars denied
For a moment, I thought
The doors hissed closed
Mockingly behind me

FOREVER BLUE

Our world's still blue
Like the Drake Hotel

The morning after
    When the San Diego winds
    Carried the scent of your perfume
    Down the winding stairs of tomorrow

MY POOR POOR CHILDREN/A POEM FOR YUSUKE

I sit with RAIN RIVER at side with thoughts of poems;
"jack" and TOWN AND THE CITY Wolfe inspired
Literary failure and imagine drunken Kerouac tears
Floating like feathers in a broken wind
The RAIN was a melodic and beautiful gift read on a
Ebon encrusted April three a.m. night of American
Madness! Madness! Madness!
Where the news earlier tonight screamed of six
Children shot at the Washington National Zoo
And I think to myself that she, Kwannon, Bosatz;
Where is love; love, love goddess of mercy
Oh how the devils [laugh and dance] deaf to the
Mexacalli blues poor poor children
You have seen Yaksha but as Kusunoki Masashige
Seven times
Seven times shall you children sing forever graced
I have held the broken wing and wept I have lived the twilight
Duel
Trice have I given and received love in rose petal softness
My being holds your being poor poor children
My eyes weep your tears
With the suchness of snow
I am the mother that suckled you my poor poor children
And today the red sun rises over love and the warmth
Burns over both hunger and the man and the woman who
Dance and lovers touch excited with passion and the warmth
continues
To burn as children born and aged cease

So my poor poor children welcome home for my tears were
Like rocks thrown at the moon
And I; I am only sand and the need for
Love and to be loved which is both my greatest weakness and strength
Under the flowing river of life
And a red rose is picked for a young lover's heart while a pink rose is placed
On freshly turned earth and the
cycle that is forever continues unbroken
As life is love my poor poor children the rains flood and feed as I cast my net
On the blue peaceful waters to touch your hand my lover on the shore
Where I first beheld your eyes, where our bodies were bound together
As the stars are fixed to the skies
My poor poor children I am the spring from whence you first arose
And today the red sun rising brings the warmth that burns over love.

My Soul

My soul is an animal
    Caught in the trap of life
    My mind is a bird
    With a broken wing

LOOK OUT DESOLATION PEAK TOUCH FORGOTTEN ANGELS LIKE CLOUDS

Be my mexacalli baby
    Yoko calling John
    Plastic Ono Band
    Railroad blues
    The hum of fireflies
    Is silence
    Beaded shades of darkness
    Lies morning
    Birds chirping in
    Mexacalli happiness
    Souls of angels
    Like sparrows gliding
    Homeward
    Freight train rumble
    Tracks going nowhere
    Everywhere on
    Mekacalli Tuesday
    Soul passing on lips
    Like gossamer web/thread
    Yeah why gone baby
    Whine mine
    Guitar line
    Couldn't dance forever
    Mexacalli
    Blues baby freight train
    Rumble
    Blow sax man

Jazz dance thunder
A quiet trumpet
Red checkered
Tablecloth clinking
Glasses band with mexacalli shades
Sultry blue She sings voice
As close as the past yeah
Billie of the strange fruit
And scars soul dripping
Poison clutching the
Mexacalli jazz/blues thing
When my mother cries
My spirit weeps the
Hoot owl whoops upon
The window ledge as
Sparrows seek their endless
Flight and I encased in wood
And glass both home and coffin make to turn
Away from her that birthed the lowly
And the great so safe within my tomb
Of locks each door and window barred
Our mother's voice upon the winds
So melancholy and sad

TUESDAY NIGHTS

Was the whiskey and the jazz playing
    On too many black nights with too
    Many lonely women and not a poem
    Between them
    How many times can you run
    From the shadow of the voices that
    Surround you
    Beating like drums in the darkness
    Tasting more of your flesh each time
    Not leaving enough for a man to breathe
    No way for a man to live
    How could the hep-cat jive survive
    When my voice can only spit silence
    Wasn't a dream left to filter thru
    The night worn inside and out and
    Bled dry a bottle singing the page blank and life in the hands of the
haves laughing at the broken shadows of the have-nots

    There was a club on 34th and Second ave. where the jazzman swung
    All night long beat poets recited Tuesdays' nights and Jack was
always drunk in the third booth
    Scrawling poems on paper bags and notebooks
    Taking life hard on the chin and after a while not fighting back
anymore
    Ain't the road that done Jack in

NEW YORK BLUE

That last day I rode the rails into the village
   Trying to hold onto the memories
   Steam rising from subway vents on crowded streets
   Hustler's doing their thing
   Chicks using babies as props to score drug money
   Gays and gangs and businessmen
   Buddhist chic and cowboys
   Coffee at a table outside of the café
   Drunken slowly, knowing I could not stay
   Knowing a part of me would never leave
   She's a nightmare, a twisted vision
   By day she paints her face and the players act
   Their parts dressed in fineries of madness
   A show for the masses
   When the night folds her cloak over
   The sun and the neon rise
   You can hear death rattle behind you as
   You walk and the real city emerges like
   The dead from their graves
   And those who are wise click there
   Deadbolts shut and hide until daybreak
   That was the whore I loved to play
   When the jazz was so real
   You could almost hear Billie singing the blues
   Nobody messed with you if you belonged
   To her and the real city was blue
   Like a fine button-down coat
   That would always keep you warm

Jazz

Nail walking down the street
    Carrying a bagful to fix something
    For the master who owns my dreaming
    Storefronts lolling sidewalks asleep
    Night quiet jazz, Erie, PA
    The endless road breaking cartons
    Locked doors being kidnapped jumping
    Fences getting spotted running away
    Dreaming snatches of words in the air
    Fine milky jazz boots on a roll a train
    That passes at 10: a.m. cars with their vapor
    Mist the chuga-chuga sound of a boxcar to
    No-where the rattling of walls when you are
    Alone hot tea Lorrianne in a skirt a poetry
    Reading in N.Y, moving out with only the
    Shirt on my back going down, back, out, taking
    Chris to the mermaid bar covered in sand, no shoes
    Living nearby close to the sea, changing
    Having enough cool to chill sand enough to scratch
    That you never itch enough life that you're full
    Digging the diz and jack going, back going, back going
    Because you want to/needing nothing 'nothing but a little
    Taste now and again just being free doing it instead of it doing you

BILLIES CROSS

I used to dance with Griselda but I always
    Had eyes for the maid. She could walk with
    The sway of Coltrane but her lips were miles
    And she knew that secret and better yet kept it
    The ratta-tat-tat to the beat
    Back in swing town when H was Billie's cross
    And the waterfront was blue like oceans on a
    Island bay
    We wore spats then, man they were the cat's
    Pajamas dressed to the nines to kill
    Griselda, my lady of poor streets
    Stayed home to dream
    Yeah man, Harry's was the spot then
    To swing wild and dig scene and dance
    And Fridays the maid would come by
    Painted with street life and free
    And the first dance would be slow
    Her eyes burning like an unattended fire
    This was our dance, our secret moment
    Swaying gently in my arms until the beat
    Moved us and we became two reckless lovers
    Drowning in the flow of whiskey's freedom
    We'd make love in the Nash, cheap and warm
    Pretending that Griseida's dreams wouldn't always come between us

TROUT LOVE

She called it love
   A cloak against the winds
   Of Ideath and loneliness
   But Brautigan and multi-colored days
   Were like a stranger to her
   There was never a trout in her dreams
   Nothing as warm as Margaret
   Between us
   It wasn't love, not like Pauline
   Not close or real not like the fine
   Berries we shared for breakfast
   She called it love but it wasn't

SNAKESKIN

MISTY as the powder of my soul
    The demi-god of legend
    Haunts like snakeskin
    Wandering my dreams
    Igniting my being
    Begging for your touch
    Smoldering my loneliness
    Forever

THE DEATH AND LIFE OF A POET

LAMENT FOR FEDERICO GARCIA LORCA
" I'm still alive!" sayeth the quote of a jailer;
Images that swim. But I didn't know him,
Only a newspaper review of the book by
Ian Gibson.
What poems do the wounds of butchered
Poets recite after fifty-three years?
In a metaphor of ice, the red cape waves;
The bull defecates the grave, the matador
Smiles.
Both thirty-eight I/him
Just the words of Richard Elman
To guide the shaft of my pen
The poem an arena of death
Danced on by gypsies.
We carve words on passing clouds
As we stand on forgotten dirt roads
Awaiting the running of the bulls
I/Him both thirty-eight
Beneath the weight of time
I listen for the song of your blood

TALKIN' WITH HERSCH

Walking with Hersch up the avenue
  b-bop cat telling me of Paris
  Ginsberg and Burroughs
  Like he's Chris C. man
  And we're heading for land
  On Crystal and coffee
  Dig the different cries
  Sirens, con men and broken
  People asking for change hard
  To tell the difference walking
  Pass eyes of despair like everywhere
  Man like everywhere you can feel the
  Heat of the street ain't a thing you can
  Do about it
  Walkin' baby babe just walkin'

I USED TO BE ABLE TO

Drop a poem like a gunslinger clearing the street
    It was easy writing of guns and hookers
    Been times when I had both in my face
    Longtime and times change
    But memories linger
    And don had me drawn
    Inches from the dealing
    Roberta was crying
    The hallway reeking of death
    But you can't run
    When you're called down
    Not when the street lays claim
    To your soul so you shimmy the max
    And don't back down and maybe you'll
    Live long enough to breathe thunder

TURNSTYLE BLUES

Once man believed the world to be square
    And I sought the horizon
    Once your words were as honey
    Your eyes shone with magic
    And I sought to be part of your life
    Once man learned that the world was a sphere
    The horizon was no longer a mystery
    Once she left and never returned
    I understood the horizon

I SMELL DEATH

It's in your soft velvet eyes
    Your lips when you think of the time
    They quiver because they know
    I smell death, it's your perfume
    And Jesse, he may as well have placed
    His own neck into the noose and jumped
    He didn't even have enough sense to wait for the
    Hangman

BUKOWSKI

Was the last of the civilized outlaws
    Back when men settled their differences
    In back alleys with their fists
    Was the last of the lovers who
    Loved whores the hard-bitten hard
    Drinking sad whiskey breath type
    Who always cry when you let
    Them stay around for awhile
    Was the last of the gamblers in a town that
    Plays it safe at the track blind bet exacta
    On the mudder neck
    Man he could have owned the place

DEMONS 1

Maybe I'll never find desolation
    Except for the loneliness of my own backyard.
    Or given the chance would I listen to the fallen angels
    Learning how to spread their wings
    Somehow it seems that I am not even safe in dreams anymore.
    Lifes' ugly tentacles reach out for me while I'm sleeping.
    They conspire with nightmares to destroy me. I hear them when
    They enter my unlocked bedroom door. Their hot breath steams
    On the back of my neck as I toss and turn. Life's night demons
    Dance on my bedpost. Their laughter can often be mistaken for the
wind
    But a few lost souls know the truth.
    The female demons all look like Julia Roberts; the men resemble
Richard
    Gere. Thy are forced to wear the masks of gargoyles. Night demons
breed
    Quickly; consume the fright of children and old men and women.
Demons hunt
    In packs during the waning of the moon. Sometimes they gather at
my bedside
    To laugh at my dreams. They weave the fallen hair of wolves into tart
tragedy
    That slithers in dreams with a life of its own. Demons light their way
by striking
    Matches on the metal thorns of the statue of Jesus over my bedside.
On nights of the
    Full moon tears falling from the statue often wake me. Once I saw a
demon bring fear
    To the face of a god. I often wonder how I survive each night and
why demons ask

Nothing of me but to be partners in the damned. I've offered them my soul but they

Only pointed the way to hell and laughed uproariously at the notion. Demons have long ago

Sawed through the gates of heaven and spent their time in hell. Now in eternal boredom

They taunt and torture men. "Nothing better to do on a Saturday night," I heard one of them

Say once.

DEMONS 2

Life never gave up a quarter
   Ain't she a bitch
   Rolling down the highway of our lives
   Morning demons line the dining room table as I drink my five-thirty
a.m. coffee.
   A pack of them stretch across the flat service and dance the can-can.
"La-da-da-da
   Da-la-da," they sing as they kick their tiny legs in unison. One races
between the crystal
   Salt and pepper shakers. It is laughing and mocking me as it climbs
into a basket of artificial
   Flowers. "Where's the booze," it yells as it pokes its demon head out.
Funny I was thinking
   The same thing. I explain to the demon that I must leave for work
even on Sunday morning.
   "Sorry no booze until this afternoon," I tell it. "Asshole," it replies. I
notice that some of the
   Demons have clung to the shaft of my umbrellar as I walk to work in
the rain. " Miserable day
   Huh, chump," the demon says as I shake my umbrellar to try and lose
them. I toss it into the
   Utility closet at work and close the door. It does me no good for as I
drink my second cup of
   Coffee I spot it. The demon climbs out of a can of Very Fine apple
juice on the lunchroom table.
   At work. Licking its lips, it taunts me. "Not bad but it will be better
when it ferments." In anger I
   Toss the non-deposit can into the garbage pail. I can hear it
scampering around the plastic

Container. The demon rattles the can until the lid of the container crashes heavily to the floor.

"Miss me," it asks as it pulls itself up to peak out. "I was hoping you wouldn't be back so soon;

What is it about me that attracts you?" " Must be your blue eyes," the demon laughs as he fades away.

"You should have left that one in the fridge a little longer," the demon says as I sip from my beer

At ten of three on Sunday. It whispers to me that we might run dry and panic licks at my lips like

The old days. The demons know I miss the needle and would go back if history could only pass

By my lonely window. When the world has closed its heart the voices of the demons are loudest.

Besides we all worship at a common grave. The demons have a deck of cards where I wear the mask of

Fools. Where the jack of hearts is torn the demon says I'm closest to the truth and wanders away

It climbs out of the keyhole in my father's desk and pulls the wool over my eyes. When I look up

It is inside the green amber of my imported beer bottle. "Hip-cup" the tiny demon sings in total

Happiness. Perhaps that is all there is to life and you do not need no Dali Rama or any demons!

"Hey wait a minute there," they all scream in unison. " Sorry, fellows," I say as I leave to face life

That I hate more than any demon. The demons scratch their talons over my digital clock

John Lennon sings an old Beatles number "I don't want to spoil the party so I'll go." The demons know all the words and sing along, "Party animal!!," one of them screams as it falls over the desk. I watch

It as it staggers over the hard wooden floors. The demon is so stoned that it's quiet as glass.

It's voice is only a shard. Distant and forlorn,Sometimes I wish I was only a demon and not a victim of Eden.

E

Darkness on the corner
  Shadows of the night;
  Winds of moonlight move the branches
  Shake dreamers who sleep late
  Park along the garage of emptiness
  Where strangers steal your car /They can't get far Not on

7 A.M. APR 29, 1990 SUN

all is silence
   all is loneliness
   Moondog my old friend
   I bet right now you have ditched Sunday service
   In heaven and are swigging down a bottle of Jack
   Daniels behind those pearly gates with Janis
   "just another piece of my heart now baby."
   Sung by a choir of angels tired of hymns.
   God sick of waiting in an empty church
   Storms out and spots Janis. He gives her a half-smile
   Half-sneer reminding her for a second of a young
   Elvis Presley, Picking up a guitar, the heavens begin to
   Rock'n'roll

LAST EXIT

I had to roll the kid out of the way to get by with the radiator enclosures.

He didn't have much left of anything from the waist down and a nurse wss

Yelling at him to turn the radio down. I knew working in a va hospital was a

Mistake but I was short on booze , luck and cash. Josie had left when the money

Went dry and betting my last check from TRUCKCASTERS on the horses didn't

Pay off. Now all I did all day was talk to those forgotten soldiers and drink in the

Utility closet. The staff dealt with me as a useful artifact, sort of like a coat rack or an

Umbrella. Something you can use sometimes but most times just ignore. I think it

Was my third week there that I met Johnny. He was a gorilla of a black man who had

Lost an arm and his eyesight trying to save some kid who paniced; charged straight

Thru a barrage of enemy fire to drag back a white kid who had hated him anyway.

I never knew or asked where he got it but Johnny turned me on to the best shit

I have ever smoked. I supplied the Jim Bean; before I got canned I snuck him into

Town with me for some drinking and some whoring. I saw him after that a few times

When I still lived in Akron but my money ran out and I had to split. A social worker

Would read him the letters I wrote and write back a reply. I was living
in Phoenix

When I found out Johnny had killed himself. I could not help but
remember his last

Letter to me as I drove to the local watering hole for the major drunk
of my career

Just as Johnny had done that final night in Akron his final letter to
me spoke of last

Exits. I hadn't understood what he meant until then. Johnny had told
me he had missed

His last exit. He said he had felt himself die that time in the war but
refused to cross over

To the other side. "My soul is gone, elliott," He would say and then
he would cry.

Tears would run down from his sightless eyes and I'd pass him the
bottle.

"Not having a soul never hurt me none," I would tell him and that
giant of a man

Would say; "Pass me that bottle, friend." Then he would laugh his
hoarse laugh

And a smile would cross his lips. Tonight drunk as usual that's the
way I want to

Remember Johnny.

GEORGE AND DAD

George Montgomery left one last beer in the fridge'

One last poem written in the sands on the dark side of the moon

Where the winds will never disturb it. Does death bother the coffin
dream we share

Like spoiled wine left too long in the summer sun? Our alleys drank
different blood

And so we never met; fell drunk on the straw mats that rested
beneath our tombstones

The numbers of our passing; flashing neon lighting up our common
grave like

MCDONALD'S over 3 billion served.

An empty can of 'BUD LIGHT' resting on the desk of my dead
father, thirty-nine years

Gone. Drunk I dance upon his gravesite as he whistles tunes off-key
from the tubular

Metal vase in the wilted ground. Perhaps as I type George and Dad
arm wrestle

Over blond angels whose shy smiles disguise the devil in their hearts

George Montgomery left one last beer in the fridge!

SOUNDS AND SONGS OF the HUMPBACK WHALES

Whales bone crunching death decay
   Their song whoop whoop gulls cry
   Along waves break repent sing whoop whoop whoop/
   They sing below the whalers/ HUMPBACK WHALES
   The cry as lonely as the deepest loneliness
   They sing in sadness and joy/ whoop/whoop/ whoop
   Waves crash drag repent break go blind and High
   Pitched yell and deep bass answer sad like the
   Whine of a puppy then they sing cacophony of
   Discordant music
   Humpback Whales /Beat poets of the seas

SOUNDS AND SONGS OF THE HUMPBACK WHALES AND JAPANESE FLUTE STORMS

They call whoop, whoop whoop below breaking waters rushing waves
　Ancient mariner sonar love cries happy/sad deepening voiced cacophonous
　　Magic whoop whoop shrill answer songs engines humming
　　Tweet Tweet wha wha wha
　　They cry deep ocean sadness
　　Below the bastard whalers
　　Curled ancient embryo so azure in your oldness
　　Close your weary eyes
　　Leave your frightened soul
　　Upon the shore of dream
　　Go to sleep though it will sadden me to say goodbye
　　Your road was hard and I may not follow
　　Sleep my aged and lonely one find the rest that life
　　Would not afford leave me only your dream to touch;
　　To embrace one last time I have no right to hold you
　　The blue silence that binds us echoes madly all around
　　Asking tears of stone faces that slowly move away
　　Flutes scale the mountain like eagles hovering
　　I walk shadowed empty rain drenched streets
　　Thunder cracks overhead
　　Trains roar by with the spidery figure of Kerouac
　　As I walk with my beer rain soaked and weary to
　　The bone my silent road is filled with vipers
　　Consuming me in boozed agony I reel
　　Lamp posts are blind before me
　　Curse me under their breath

I am fire consumed desolation
Without a poem to bear my name

PIERCING THE NIGHTENGALE SMOOTHNESS

Rejected work is too beat 90's poetry editor tells me
    Afraid of Kerouac the only comparison between us the
    Blood and my worn and tired liver
    Ain't seen no road nor Sal or Dean
    Jazz played soft and blue
    The honky-tonks have all moved past
    Those days are now all through
    That hep-cat jazz was the end, man
    Blues drenched horn swinging from
    The bandstand a little blow to help
    Go and dig the scene Chershire grinned
    88 man layin' down some boogie
    Cats and their ladies prowling the
    Weekend night neon and flesh everywhere
    Baby far gone smokey coffeehouses as real
    As Texas sawdust
    Jack and Allen and their jazz poems
    Piercing the nightingale smoothness
    With howls and Sal too real for the
    Whitebread

FOR MERLE

Those forties cats had a beautiful rap
    Breathing whiskey breath poems
    Where the fluxs was the cruxs of the matter
    The matter and the dreams were madhatters
    Dreams like Alice fucking by the looking glass
    And rabbits staring into the mirror smacking
    Their lips at the cave/pussy stretched between
    Alice's thighs and jack clould a' stood at that scene
    Writing a blues drenched sparrow of a jazz
    Night throwing up putting down eating from a
    Heated spoon the candle a wordless poem resting
    Against the tired night on the branches of our lives
    But digging it like heaven from a whiskey glass
    That only our livers protest the rest never given but
    Taken
    Lean on the bar rail eyes closed jack
    Float downstream while time melts away the
    Lonely hours escape the touch of death's despair
    Gaze pass silver flowers
    Take a pill, a drink, a shot
    Forget even what or who you are
    Tie your mind into a knot
    Make it pretty like a Christmas present
    Maybe I shouldn't have bought ya that last drink
    The one that done ya' in
    But I drank it first and bled but never gave it no mind
    Jus' kept scrawling poems on the wings of dead birds
    I ain't never guessed man did not know your face or
    Who you were my own mirror cracked, spitting dripping
    Down the walls music swelling on the morn of Friday

I tasted it but never understood
Brood for me baby and lay your tired eyes on my soul

NEW YORK CITY BLUES

[A Poem Written On 8th Avenue And 41St St As I Spoke with Herschel Silverman]

YEAH the city sometimes it's like Cannonball and Miles playing autumn leaves and

Sometimes it's something altogether different dig the mob sounds in the background

As we stand in the 850 parking garage saying "Hey I think it's a movie!" yeah like

Me or a ghost of me past at seventeen left for dead in Queens car wrapped

Around a elevated cement railroad embankment too much jazz to go like give me

One for Daddy-O- but please I'm just a kid just let me live and dig it they did the

Flash is past and Dave is loading unsold books into the back of his Volvo from the

Small press convention in ny. Ana is pulling her parka tighter like a trumpet going outstream

To beat the rhythm. She is correct you can feel the groping of the cold wind like un-wanted

Hands in the darkness. I dig them all the most they are somethin' else but Ana turns to listen

To the mob in the distance and I flash dance into the bitter past Yeah the heat dig it's early

Seventies and I am at Downing stadium just groovin' on Hendrix, the Woodstock thing baby

But the black panthers and the young lords have taken over the concert retitled it; "free"

47

For the people like a revolutionary thing but dig someone wants my fringed vest and I'm like

Freaked mickeyed with a mix of strychnine and lsd and this ain't some Alison's Uncle but a

Real bad mutha' and we're both thrown into the east river but I peak and see god and the end

Of the world and maybe the airplane were playin' but there is pollution everywhere

Baby and I'm chokin' in it/ can't even fuckin' breathe and I feel myself start to die and

Those who knew me then would say I did but that was where ELLIOTT was born in that

Jazz drenched tornado storm but dig sometimes I miss the dead and the city leaves me with

Bad vibed NEW YORK CITY BLUES

FOR DAVE CHRISTY AND ANA
WITHOUT WHOM

Allen Ginsberg eyes
  Puked anal truth
  Small press conventon and I withdrawn without
  Withdrawal listened raptured too shy to ask
  His autograph or even speak Huncke reading
  Of jail and junk and fixing
  Me flashing backwards fetal position on the sidewalk
  Needing a fix so bad I would have licked the devil's
  Asshole to tie up just one more time
  Friend Herschel Silverman's beautiful words
  Full of life and truth without the ugliest of scars
  Weighing like a raven in the poe-drenched night
  And Corso child Corso going pee-pee paper cupped
  Mad man of beat wildness with Kerouac's demon
  Perched on his drooped shoulder
  Saddened my heart the boxer, the fighter John
  Winers wavering on the podium like ancient
  Ali between rounds and vultures smacked their lips
  But I wanted to cheer to catch his thick eyeglassed
  Eyes and SCREAM "One more round champ!"
  Yeah dig it for me and Herschel and Allen and
  Herbert—-—"one more round champ!"

ALLEN GINSBERG'S EYES

Poems From The Small Press Book Fair Part 2
And smack from the devil's cup once seared my veins
Weed' needs too much speed
Like Corso 2 my liver laughs
Cause when I shit I bleed
I know you've been in prison
But when the cop caught me
It was near the end of the midnight shift
And so he set me free with two bags of
Junk and some coke
Had luck like good jazz when I was younger
And damn life was different higher
Had no idea; dig
Now Ginsberg at the reading made
Me think yeah dig and Huncke well he brought
It all home fixing with bikers in my sister's bedroom
George the junkie ripping off my mother's sterling
Silver; wouldn't mind except I didn't get
A fuckin' dime
Hey I was never no Kerouac or no Corso
I stumbled into heroin before I died and rose in the
Ashes of New York city the phenix Elliott
Bled shell dead soul bleeding into every crack
That ran into the sewers and I never could dance
But baby I could take the chance hitting the plunger
Of the hypo into heaven sucking nirvana thru my
Viens my eyes exploding 4th of July ecstasy
A SPEEDBALL
Junk and coke shot bent needle death not caring never

Any further than the nearest exit
The door as barred as hell itself

ALLEN GINDSBERG'S EYES SMILE ON HERSCHEL SILVERMAN

Small Press Book Fair Poem Part 3
YEAH I can't remember if we met but Herschel is giving the first reading
and he is good but the crowd to me don't give him no warmth and he's
reading something called; NEW YORK I think my mind so shot by acid
I can't recall but he's good and I like his poems before I meet him which
makes it cool cause I don't dig to lie but like I am gone man gone and
just dig him and the hand he gets is good and I clap loud dig the vibes
all around me Corso gives the crowd Corso clever beat and funny and
gets what he wants in return dig it just watching him I sense it; this jive
be-bop cat needs to be loved I sense it all around him from the whiskey
in his cup to the sadness hidden in his eyes. The cheering crowd a father
to his mind

Allen's gentle kiss upon

Gregory's cheek does not prepare me for his words float without
coats in the cold without ladies no

Government with gates has freedom and I dig his wisdom

His vision and his smile as he works the crowd into a frenzy and
Huncke takes me back to junk and

Smiles and Richard Brautigan

More blood from my nose than torn up veins and John Weiners
sweet John mumbling his words

Of travel like a sailor lost from home masturbating in Naples with a
newsreel of Clark GABLE and I want

John to come out of the corner dancing the Ali shuffle but I settle for
the warmth of the crowd and

Try to sustain the crowd applause

John I want to chew the age from you and spit it at the crowd Hold
the salivated pieces up to the sky

Saying Jesus kiss my ass but I am silent but not on this page baby
cause without a soul it's all
That elliott's got left
Dig the need the feed the speed all the things the homeless need

SMALL PRESS BOOK FAIR PART4

TWO days after saying goodbye to Ana, Dave and Herschel I'm hungover

And feeling seedy not near to the realization of godhood as the fact that I haven't changed

My underwear since Saturday and it's Tuesday morning. So off I go to the basement

To reclaim but alas tis not dry. I check the lint trap and man oh man ain't nobody

Cleaned that sucker in ages, nothing to do in the basement of suburbia but stare

Out of the window and onto the tree lined streets where I imagine Allen Ginsberg

Sadly shaking his poem filled head

Thinking of New York one legged man staring at the penn station steps like the

Himalayas, ancient hippie of sixties memory with for sale sign by his feet on the

Sidewalk leaning/lying back against storefront wall legs spread across

Hindus, gays, hookers In shorts cold wind skyscrapers and neon new York alive

In its myriad misery

Can still hear her singing two days after reading Herschel Silverman's cool beat

Poetry at the convention table wanting to say; 'hey man you're great.' He's the first reader and this is my first time at a reading

A POEM WRITTEN FOR CEHSOIKOE IN A BAR

We moved as far down the road as life would allow
   Tried to follow Dean and Sal to San Francisco
   Somehow my angels turned out to be thinly
   Disguised desperadoes.
   I wonder as I pull off the highway which of us truly died first
   You of cocaine lips and saddened eyes
   On the road you were so young'
   Somehow we never touched choosing for unknown reasons to
always wait for tomorrow
   Now you are five years gone to whatever highway lies beyond us
   And tonight a light rain falls on the highway
   I have followed Sal and Dean and Dave and Ana
   To a bar where my beer sits next to sunglasses[purple]
   And a wolf waits patiently, Holding a pool cue like an erection
   She follows me into the back room. I drag too deeply on a pall mall
   And drink my last one much too quickly.
   Her eyes are honeyed and a little sad. I am drunk and tell her she
   Should have been a Mexican. She brings out the coke and we descend
   A little further into death. Morning roars in the distance like a
   Forgotten pagan god demanding worship. The rain beats down but
   Never cleanses the street as I stagger home spitting oblivion into
   The gutter.

HORSES

I hit the stream and feel the rush, Roxanne, [Diane's stage name and who she is when stoned]

Sets up a couple of lines Tonight she is warm and the wind blows in loudly from off the coast

By Long Beach New York. Eddie, Diane's husband has passed out on the sofa, beer can in hand

She is beautiful and I love her but will not know it until cocaine drives a stake through her heart

And they call me at work to tell me she is dead

Tonight we have two more years together and the ocean breaks as we lie in the coolness of the

Midnight sands. She never knew me as Elliott even after twenty or thirty lines. Sometimes from

The topless dancing at the clubs she would return bitter like poorly cut coke.

I remember crawling on our bellies through her apartment once when she didn't have enough

Shit to get whoever was at the door high also. Sometimes we would hold each other and know

That time would somehow not be enough We were stone touched lovers like Romeo and Juliet

Riding horses on the beaches at midnight, daring the world to just try and stop us.

I was younger then, listening to you talk of wanting to adopt a child. What plans we

Both had beneath the stars as we turned our eyes from heaven. Stoned we could

Hide together from this ugly world and never return. We had the wind and the ocean

And we were free under cover of moonlight to love.

Why then were we always afraid? Why didn't your lips taste different
that last night
Together? Walking home alone, where were the horses?

FATAL EXCESS

Heroin and Cocaine and Lorri Jackson And Me
We use ta cop up in south Harlem at 3 in the morning. Ted said they had the best dope

I was the only fucker that the city pigs wouldn't bother even after the spic ripped us off

And did the shit and split.

I never shot straight junk like Lorri. I always mixed it with coke for a better high.

Lenny Bruce said it was like kissing God. I dug what Paul Hoover said about flesh in excess

But when you hit your mind lit up like fireworks in flashes of a zillion colours with pins and needles

Up and down your prick would feel hot like you cummed with a beautiful movie star;

Like kissing God. Maybe Lorri's best poem was the last high, maybe her soul screamed

And sang and spit out poems drenched in vomit and excess.

Maybe she regurgitated heaven.

THE SESSION

Once again I find myself in this room
    Seven voices round a circle
    I tried to talk you out of coming here
    Earlier but you came anyway. Now
    All I can do is make you miserable.
    Only tell them what I let you, nothing more
    You do not wish to be here anymore than I do
    Always remember that. They do not know about
    Me, that is our secret and our strength. We watch
    The clock together like a key left in a cell door
    The voices around us and surround us only make
    It worse. One week ago you said something and the
    Voices of the seven were silent.
    They didn't know it was you who spoke and I who
    Was silent. In a room filled with seven voices all wait
    For the voice of the eighth.

SEVEN

Someone once said that the answer to the meaning of life is the number seven.
The totality of my existence is an odd number,
Well I could have told you that!
I don't know what the poet around the corner does but I clean toilets.
This I feel gives me the greater motivation. Drunk on pulque I fall
Face down in the gutter outside the bar near the bay of Campeche.
A Canadian tourist picks my pocket as I vomit in the alley. He cuts me
With the blade in his hand when I stumble near him. My faith restored
For the moment I paint a message on the wall of the alley in my blood.
The men from the canteen quail from the sight of my blight. A siren
Begins to scream in my brain. The gendarme stands next to me as I die,
A deputy quietly talking to him. {What did he write on the wall?"
The gendarme says to him in French.] "The totality of my existence
Is an odd number," the deputy answers him.
"Well I could have told you that!" the gendarme said
Someone once said that the answer to the meaning of life is the
Number seven.

CLOSED EYED DRIFTER

I did not see the wound or feel the blood;
    Closed eye drifter
    Beaten as a child I never felt the warmth of fire; cold
    Mother says life will curse me Never will amount to
    Anything. Father would come home drunk, take off
    His belt and beat me raw, With each unmarked grave
    I bury a scar from the past. A girl I picked up in Texas
    Used to laugh. When I cut I always close my eyes.
    One even looked a lot like dad. He, I buried all
    Alone with the last of the childhood that remained for me.
    I did not see the wound or feel the blood; closed eye drifter

SEPTEMBER 8TH 1985

Candy [not her real name] lives in Suffolk county. She is sixteen and has a taste for rock, a form of cocaine. Her older brother Phil was killed in Viet Nam when she was only four weeks old. 1969 is a year they do not mention in her home. It is the year Phil died and the year her father hung himself in the basement. Her mother drowns a little bit mote each day in the bottle. Candy lost her job at the 'PIZZA HUT' and now pays for her habit by selling herself around Oyster Bay about a mile and a half from the harbor. She tells herself and her best friend Judy that it is only until the right 'man' comes along and takes her to California where things will be different. I picked her up hitch-hiking along the off-ramp to the expressway and she never stopped talking the entire time it took us to drive to the motel. I guess I'm writing this poem about her out of guilt or maybe it's because I recognized her name in the obituary column in NEWSDAY this morning

SURVIVAL PART 1

A Message to Sharks

A message to sharks
    About survival in the nineties
    Cut out of granite and
    Hung around my neck
    "what would you call it?"
    This poison kiss of poverty
    My life drips from the faucet
    Of my soul. "will you drink of my cup?"
    Listen to the silence in madness?
    Cut it in two with anger?
    Make change with the splinters
    I died just moments before you
    Read this. Fell silent into the
    Womb of eternity until I was handed the bill.
    Needing perfection to redeem the coupon of my soul
    I return to finish this page and go to sleep.

SURVIVAL PART 2 THE DREAM

THIRD world knocking at my door
    Don't let them in
    Can't feed one more
    Wings of vultures
    Fan our love
    Eat the tongues of eagles for desert.
    Numbers run like speeding cars
    On the freeway of our souls
    Stir the gate; the burning womb
    Passing billboards as we travel with
    A message to sharks

SURVIVAL PART 3

The Dream

The echo of the scream
   Resounds in the corners of my mind
   Fills the empty corridors of night
   With the flutter of bat wings.
   She lies by my side in REM;
   Unaware of terror.
   Dreaming of children playing in the
   The snow; she smiles
SURVIVAL PART 3
THE DREAM CONT'd
   Touching the warm barrel of the pistol
   I pull the trigger on an empty chamber.
   The faceless stranger moves closer; smiling
   Bats circle overhead, the cry of their flight
   Mixing with the screaming of my soul.
   She turns, moves closer;
   Touches me lightly with her hand.
   The stranger vanishes into dust.
   The alarm clock rings.

SURIVAL PART 4

Punching the time clock of life
  I view the sharks as they continue
  To circle. Melting the iceberg of
  Loneliness with their fins they warm
  THEMSELVES ON THE BEACHES OF
  FROZEN DESIRE.
  There's a cold breeze blowing
  Shards of misery across the land
  The souls of butchered martyrs ride
  Towards the dawn wrapped in catacombs
  Of ash.

SURVIVAL PART 5 [THE ELEVATOR]

OUTSIDE a curtain of sunlight envelops
The dew of morning. The elevator that I ride plunges, vortex; vertigo,
Spinning downward floor by floor.
Below my feet the elevator has turned to glass. I view the fins of
Sharks as I continue to fall. It jolts to a halt just yards short of the
bottom.
Sharks crash their snouts into the clear glass and I fall back against
the wall.

SURVIVAL PART 6 HAIGHT ASHBURY

SLIPPING into unconsciousness I revisit haight ashhbury.
Jimi Hendrix is playing LIKE A ROLLING STONE ON the backs
of
Smiling sharks. Notes blaze in colors on streets of water.
The music rises in intensity and the sharks are driven to
Frenzy. Slowly a turbaned man rises from the sidewalk.
Raising a flute to his lips he plays " sunny Goodge street"
Jimi nods his head in thanks to Donovan. The sharks come
To a halt and smile.

SURVIVAL PART 6
HAIGHT ASHBURY CONT'D

Six drown making Donovan very sad.
    The music stops and I stir on the floor
    Of the elevator. Rising haltingly to my feet
    I press the button for the uppermost floor.

SURVIVAL PART 7 [THE TOP LEVEL]

I step out of the elevator onto the top level.
    The walls are clear and black clouds press
    Angrily against them. Pressure builds and begins to form cracks
    Blood starts to run between the
    Modernistic paintings inspired
    By Pablo Picasso. My vertigo
    Begins to worsen and as I
    Sink to my knees I notice a worm
    Begin to eat through a painting
    Of an apple near a vase on a
    table, the flowers in the vase begin
    To wilt. Petals fall on the jasper
    Carpeted hallway.

SURVIVAL PART 7

Top Level Contd
   I stare as the flowers once again bloom, then
   Fold up in rapid succession and bloom again.
   The worm crawls from the apple and begins
   To drink the blood running so freely from
   The cracks.

SURVIVAL PART 8 [THE MAN IN THE RED HOOD]

Gathering the limits of my strength
    I stagger to my feet. I lean on
    The wall moving inch by inch
    Toward the open maw of the elevator
    A man in a red hood with the face of a
    Shark asks me when I enter;
    "What floor sir?"
    I sink to my knees as I watch the doors close
    Blood begins to seep through the black
    Rubber molding of the elevator.
    I close my eyes and listen to the hum
    Of the engines.

SPACE THE FINAL FRONTIER

Oblivion's maw black hole avenger
    Voyager one plowed through my heart
    Wishing
    Beer cans stain the stable sands
    Leave a trace of tears in the wind
    On
    Tread not upon the soul of infinity
    As light below space vanish; exist
    A
    Ebb slowly gossamer shadows of venus
    Let not the moment leave without me like a
    Star

HOWLING INTO THE NINETIES

Witness thinking insanity blessed
   Unclothed ragman cry
   Staggering the back alleys of Harlem
   Shooting horse mixed with coke
   Till I think that I'll die
   My bloods been bonded
   My soul's been sold
   The highest bidder
   Let it ride
   Scarlet rivers run down the sides of
   Huge skyscrapers to drown the poor.
   In a strange brew of isolation and
   Loneliness I gasp for air.
   We stand naked and inviting
   Unfettered by the pope
   Fists turned to armor
   Howling into the nineties

THE LAKE

I'll meet you by the lake. You can tell it's me by
  The blood red suitcase at my side. Inside will be
  The fragments of my life. They are held together
By the web of doubt.
The words we will say are meaningless.
No-one will remember anyway. The
Water will be the only witness. I
Know by the rise of the dawn you'll
Be gone. I'll walk quietly to the lake
And discard the contents of my
Suitcase. When I can't stand the
Loneliness anymore; I'll get on the bus and go home.

NOT ANOTHER JACK KEROUAC POEM

Not many people know this but jack Kerouac and Elvis Presley were the same person.

You can tell by their dusted mantel majesty and the fact that their sepulchral never

Rested but was hung out on a pedestal for the chosen to worship. My coffin as

Tourist bait for the greedy. [is he talking about me?]

We wrote their epitaphs in the watered down ink of our blood.

Here lies [insert name] like a quarter peep show in a back room in

Times square red light heaven.

"Cost you more if you want to touch," she says smiling.

Not many people know this but jack Kerouac and Elvis Presley

Were the same person.

SPIRIT VENTURES

I followed along the riverbank watching the ducks frolic in the dirty
    Waters. I must be getting old for I remember them green-blue and
    And clear. A young child laughs as I skim a stone half of the way to
    the other side. I smile to myself and throw another stone. I was only
    Sixteen when I was last here and tonight I'm thirty-seven and can
    Only write about it. The thunderstorm outside prevents my going
    So only my spirit ventures out tonight.
Just for a second I recall times my younger sister; Patti
And I would stand together in the garage watching the lightning
And hearing the thunder and rain. It must be close to ten years
Since I last saw her. I wonder when it rains if she also recalls
Childhood. Childhood and old age both pass too quickly.
Some of my youth I still visit but a lot requires fast forward if you
Know what I mean. I guess everyone's life is like that. The traffic
Lights hang up from the sky like a beacon guiding my long sojourn.
I take long walks at night and at night they have friendlier faces
Then during the day. You'll have to take my word on this. However
It is true. I move forward along the sidewalk staring at the green
And red lights up ahead. I pretend that they are goals in life to be
Reached. Good I have reached my first goal. Then I pretend the
Light way up ahead is a great wish like winning the lottery or
Becoming famous. However, it is easier reaching that traffic light
Than becoming famous or winning the lottery. You have to take
My word on this. However it is true.
I can't say for sure if the traffic lights are friendlier in the rain.
This is because I rarely walk in the rain. I take a bus but don't worry I
always put it
Back[ha-ha] I wish sometimes I could walk for miles in the rain and
stay dry. I like

77

The feeling rain leaves when it drips down your back. Life is like the rain, you can

Like it but it doesn't have to like you back. That's okay though; you'll have to take my word on it.

THE POOL OF BLOOD

In the humid heat of September, I wait on the bus-stop
    For hurricane Hugo talking to a veteran who I barely knew
    Behind his dark glasses brewed a storm
    Darker and more violent than any of nature
    The VC had never landed a blow yet I could see
    The deep wounds that continued to bleed
    Looking down on my shirt
    I stared at the pool of blood from my
    Self-inflicted wounds, together we talked
    No-one seeing the pool of blood that gathered
    By our feet
    He told me that he had been sick
    There was a hospital band on his wrist
    I wondered if he could see the pool of blood
    As clearly as I could.
    Maybe he did because he looked up to heaven we spoke, we sat apart
on the bus but after
    A time he came over and sat in front of me
    Not wanting to talk we exchanged few words
    When I left the bus he only said two words
    "Stay indoors."
    "I will" I answered.
    Leaving the bus; I turned to look his way one more time
    But he was staring out of the window into his own
    Private world. I can't help but wonder how many people'
    Are killed in the war without bullets. "Goodbye my friend,"

Table of Contents